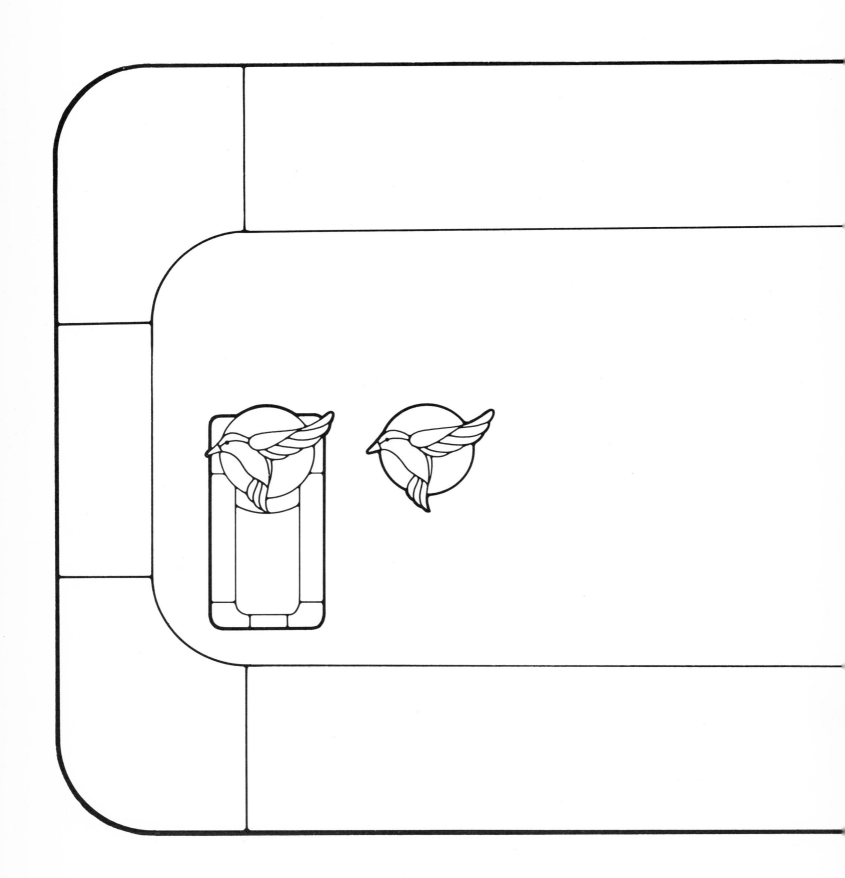

PLATE 1 (left)

Remove staples to see and use full template.

PLATE 2 (left)

Remove staples to see and use full template.

PLATE 3 (left)

Remove staples to see and use full template.

PLATE 4 (left)

Remove staples to see and use full template.

PLATE 5 (left)

Remove staples to see and use full template.

PLATE 6 (left)

Remove staples to see and use full template.

PLATE 7 (left)

Remove staples to see and use full template.

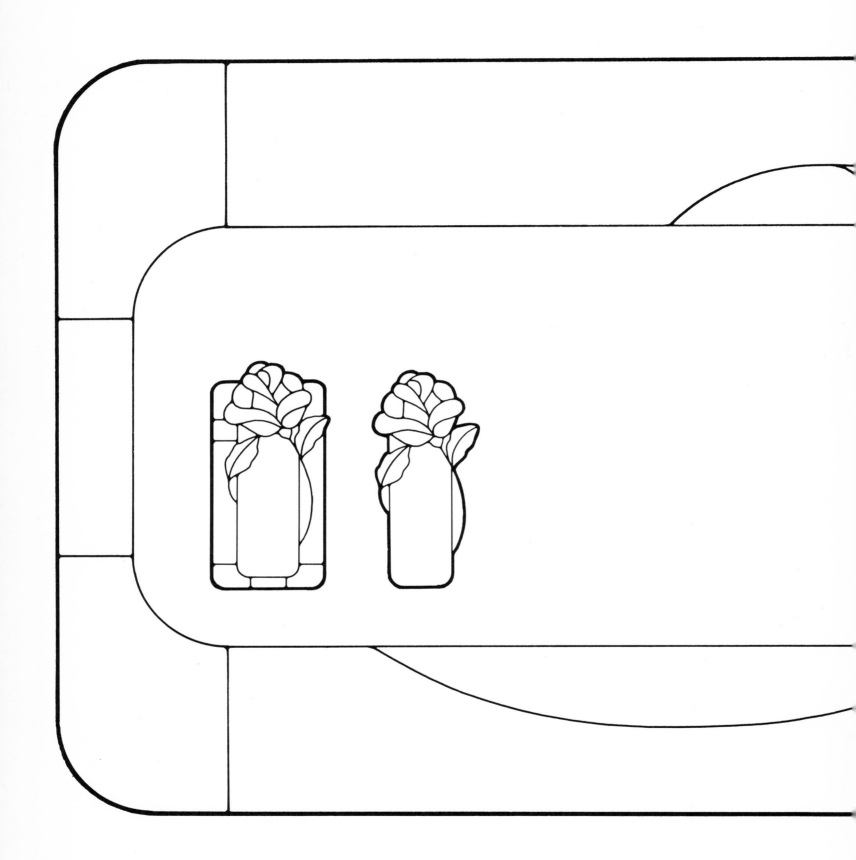

PLATE 8 (left)

Remove staples to see and use full template.

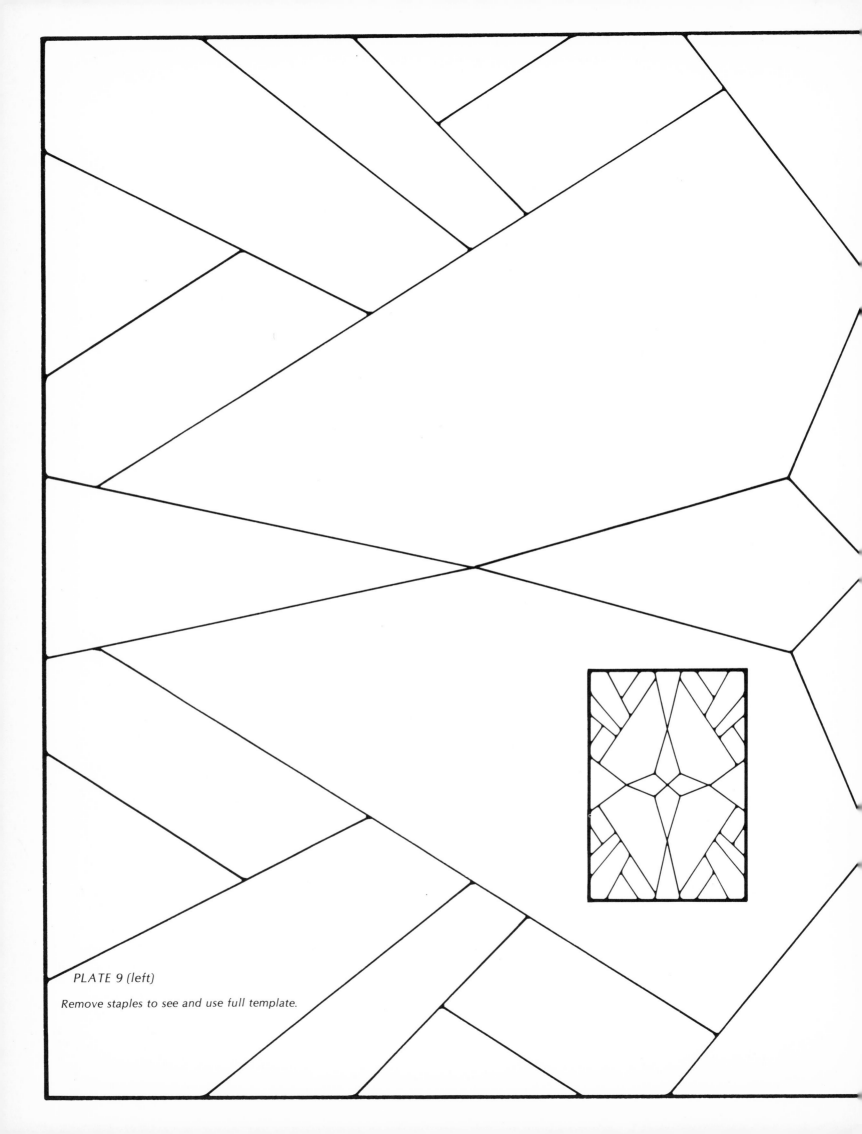

PLATE 9 (left)

Remove staples to see and use full template.

PLATE 10 (left)

Remove staples to see and use full template.

PLATE 11 (left)

Remove staples to see and use full template.

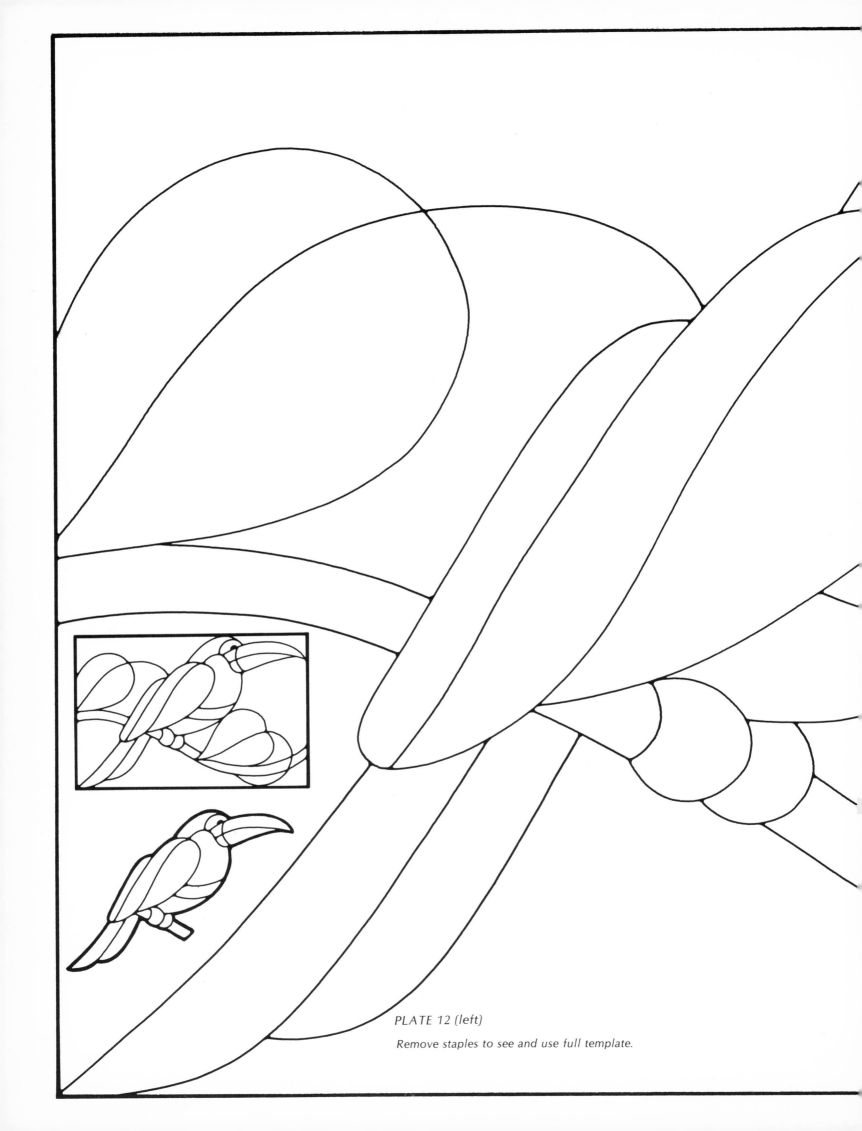

PLATE 12 (left)

Remove staples to see and use full template.

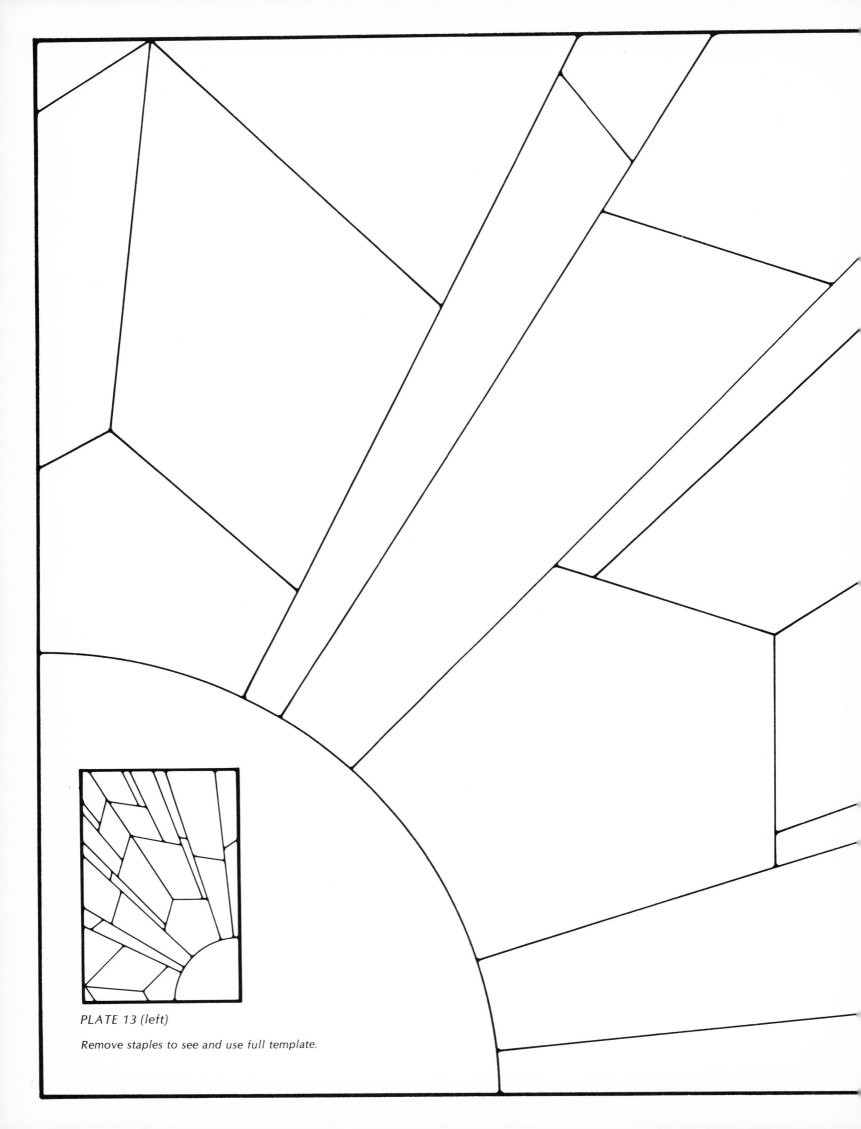

PLATE 13 (left)

Remove staples to see and use full template.

PLATE 14 (left)

Remove staples to see and use full template.

PLATE 15 (left)

Remove staples to see and use full template.

PLATE 16

Remove staples to use template.

Remove staples to use template.

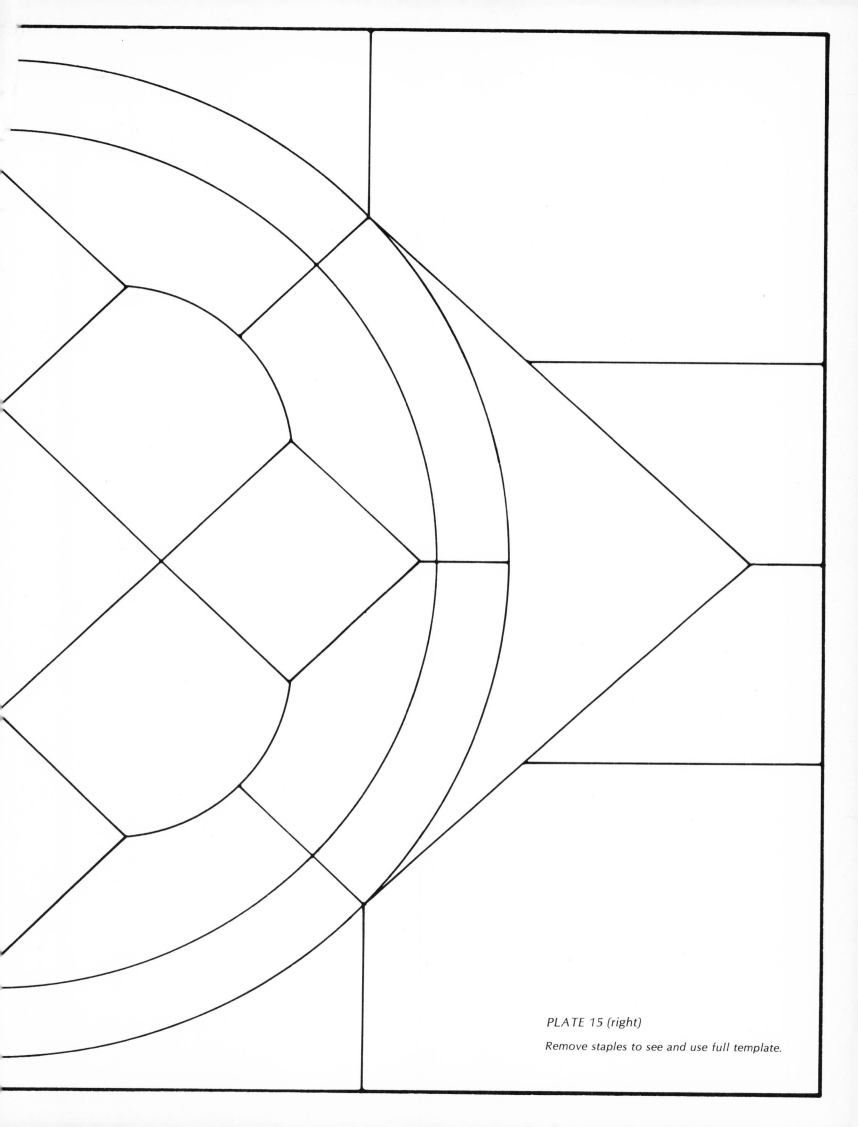

PLATE 15 (right)

Remove staples to see and use full template.

PLATE 14 (right)

Remove staples to see and use full template.

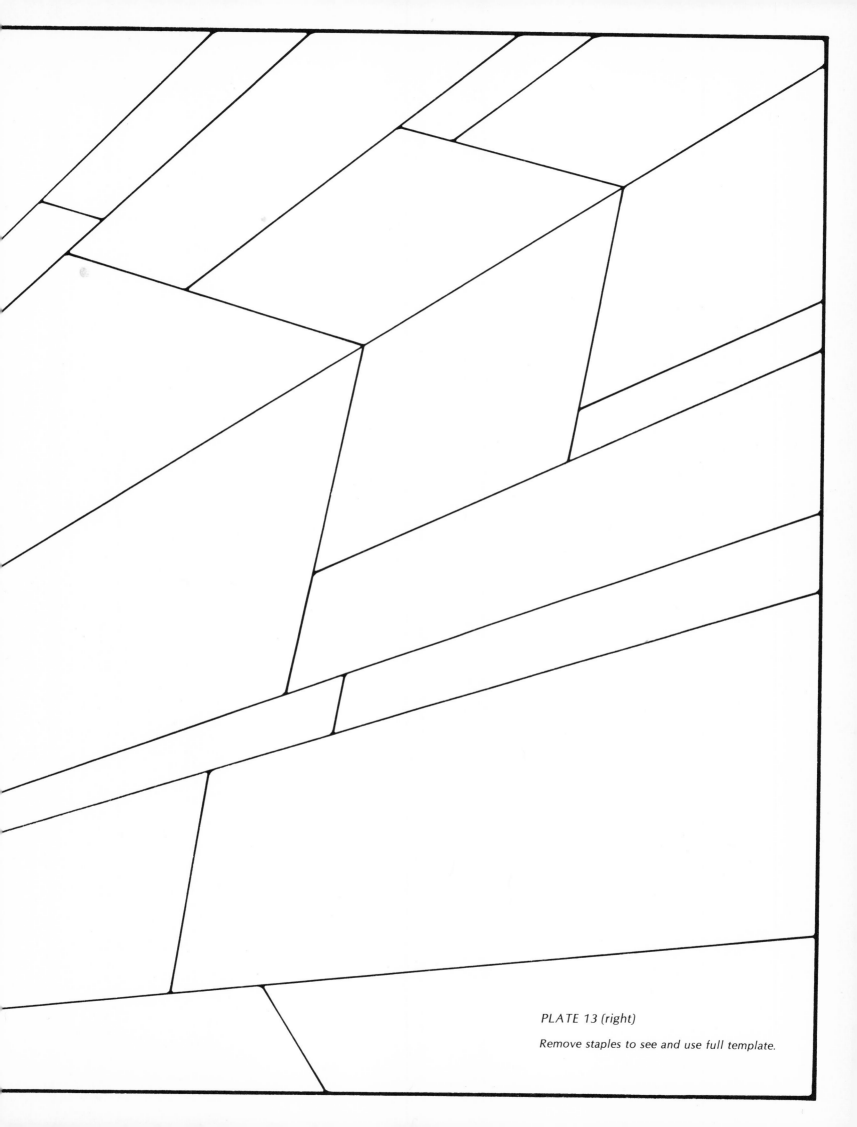

PLATE 13 (right)

Remove staples to see and use full template.

PLATE 12 (right)

Remove staples to see and use full template.

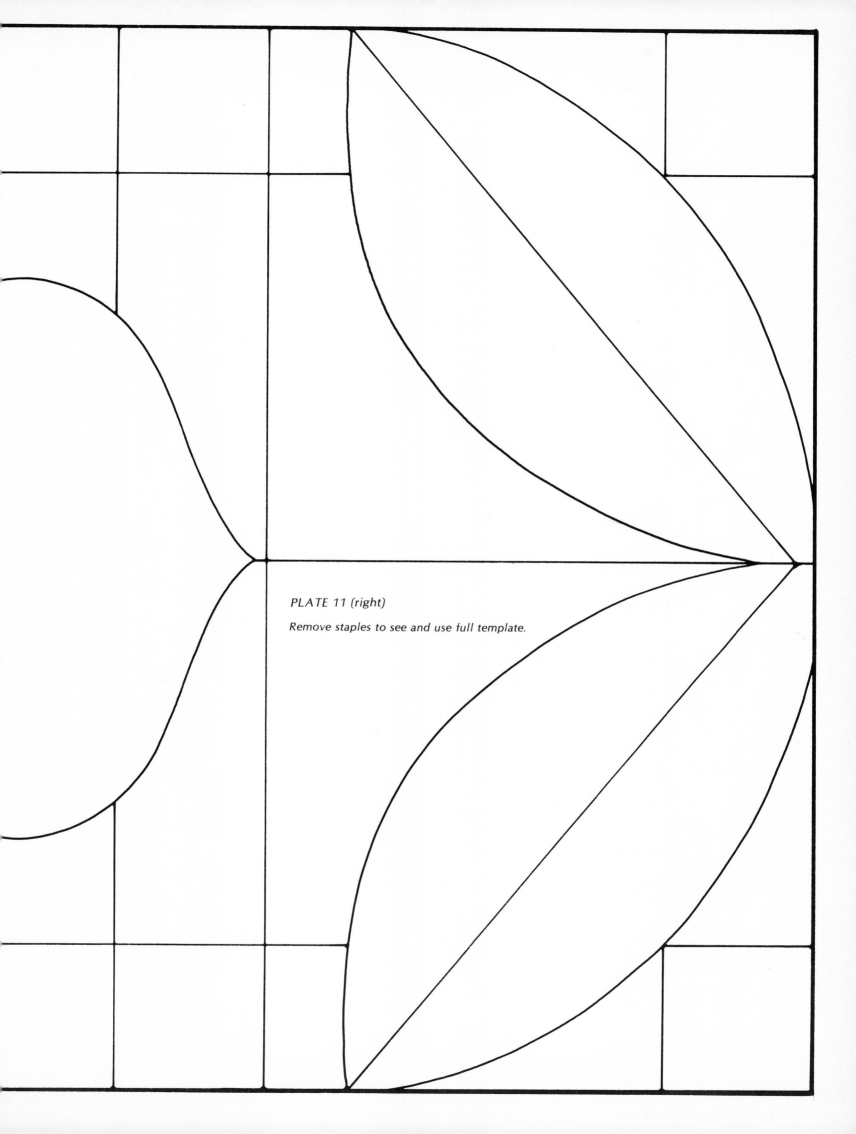

PLATE 11 (right)

Remove staples to see and use full template.

PLATE 10 (right)

Remove staples to see and use full template.

PLATE 9 (right)

Remove staples to see and use full template.

PLATE 8 (right)

Remove staples to see and use full template.

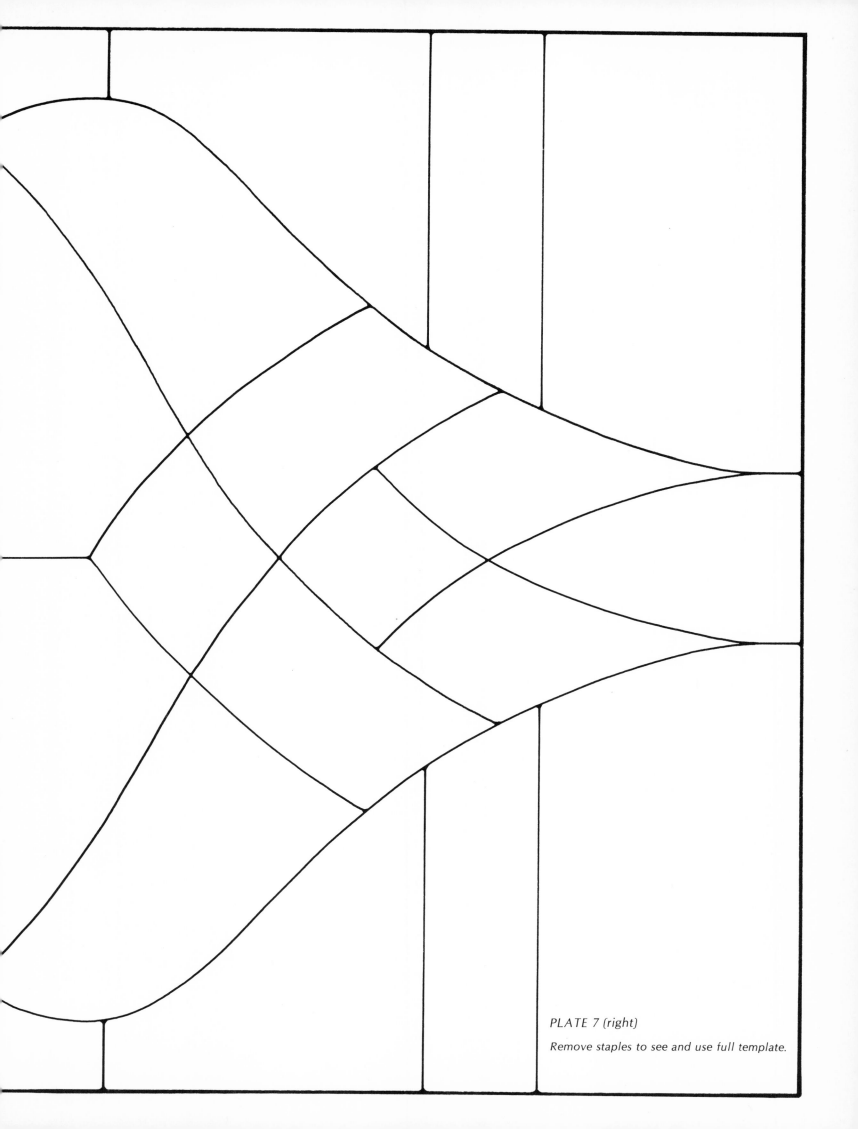

PLATE 7 (right)

Remove staples to see and use full template.

PLATE 6 (right)

Remove staples to see and use full template.

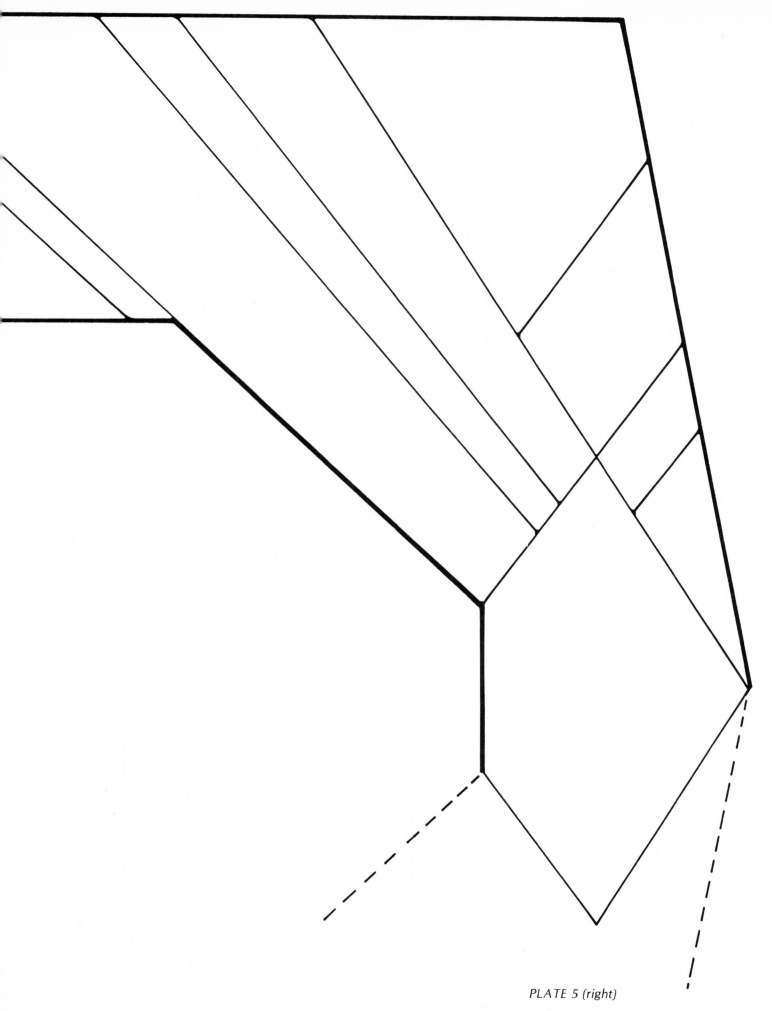

PLATE 5 (right)

Remove staples to see and use full template.

PLATE 4 (right)

Remove staples to see and use full template.

PLATE 3 (right)
Remove staples to see and use full template.

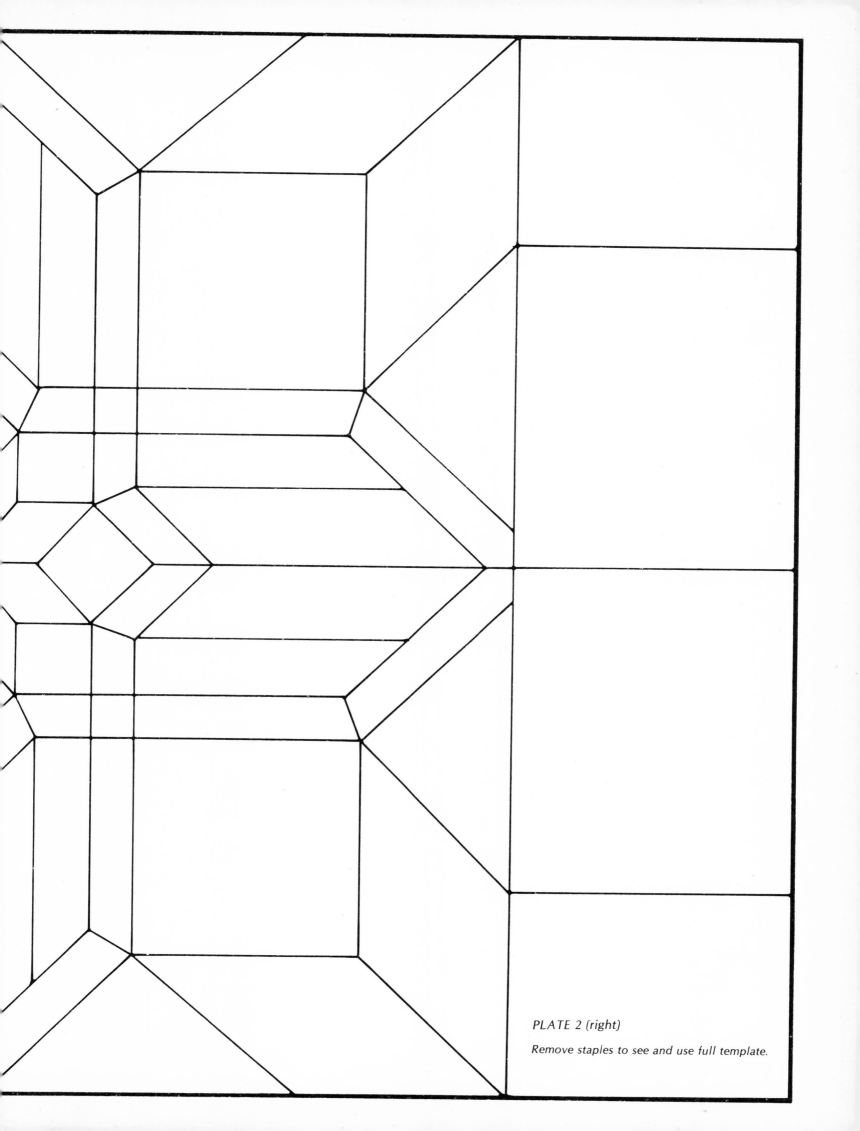

PLATE 2 (right)

Remove staples to see and use full template.

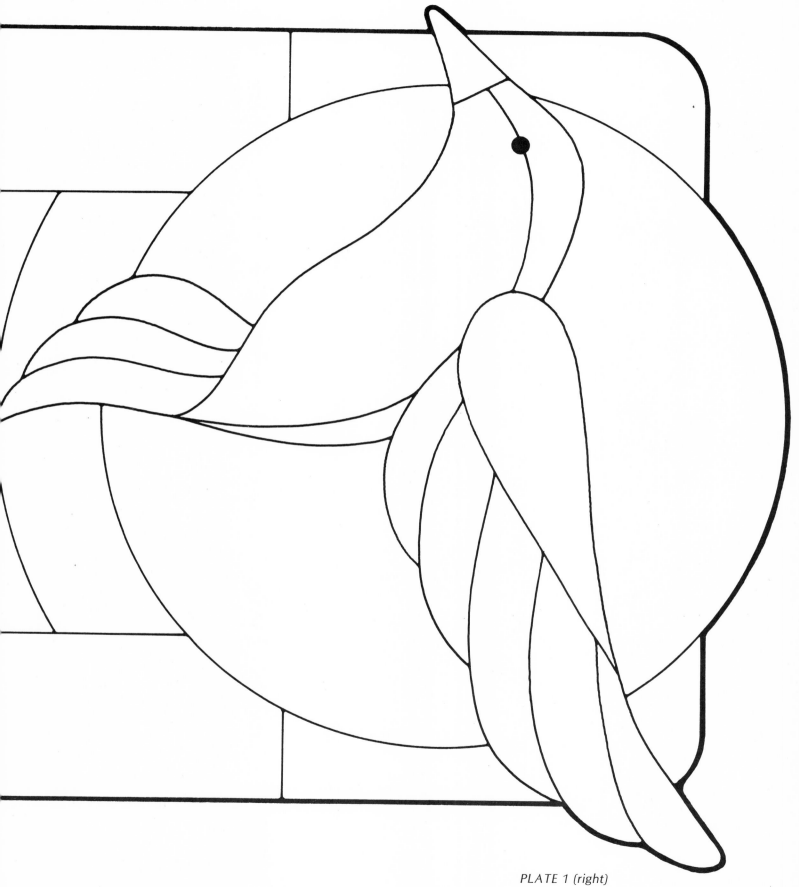

PLATE 1 (right)

Remove staples to see and use full template.